MW00749207

GOD ON THE JOB

God's Probe in Job

JOYCE JUNGCLAUS

ILLUSTRATIONS BY
MATTHEW JUNGCLAUS

◆ FriesenPress

Suite 300 - 990 Fort St
Victoria, BC, V8V 3K2
Canada

www.friesenpress.com

ISBN
978-1-03-910487-7 (Hardcover)
978-1-03-910486-0 (Paperback)
978-1-03-910488-4 (eBook)

Religion, Biblical Biography, Old Testament

Distributed to the trade by The Ingram Book Company

DEDICATION

This book is dedicated to Holy Spirit:
Helper, Comforter and Guide,
and to all who wonder why bad
things happen to good people.

TABLE OF CONTENTS

PROLOGUE
"WHY?"

Why do bad things happen to good people? It's a question written large over this world. And it was written very large over Job. God himself says, in effect, there is no one like Job on earth! He honours God and turns away from evil. And so, "Why, God?" Why would you not only allow Job's horrendous suffering, but actually orchestrate it? In most people's minds, that makes God very bad. It seems to preclude any deeper thinking—any quest to search out the question—about this dilemma, any serious efforts to unravel the mystery. If God is good, WHY? This question is worthy of being asked, and worthy of a good answer. Could there ever be a reason good enough for all this carnage?

In this look at the Book of Job, we will see several spotlights: one on Job for the devil; one on God for Job; one on the devil for Job; and one on Job's three friends, Eliphaz, Bildad, and Zophar.

This good man, Job, made in the image of God, was brought to the place of cursing himself through the severity of trials. He shook his fist, as it were, at God and said God denied him justice. He also cursed a group of young people who were mocking him by calling them fools.

In the end, there is another spotlight focusing on the "Goel," the kinsman Redeemer. It is a recognition of whose hand is in all this.

Ultimately, this true-life drama can be seen taking place as much in an operating theatre as on a stage.

CHAPTER 1

The First Spotlight:
On Job—The Stage Is Set

The Scenes Behind the Scenes: Parts 1 and 2
SCENE 1

> There was a man in the land of Uz whose name *was* Job; and that man was blameless and upright, and one who feared God and shunned evil. (Job 1:1)

The Bible says Uz was a son of Shem, so Uz was a person who had land named after him. Job was a descendant of Abraham through Shem, a Semite, who lived in the land of Uz. There is a humorous application for English speakers because Uz simply sounds like "us." And although Job, with his great prosperity, would perhaps equal a modern-day multimillionaire, his great trial is not foreign to people like us.

Job was a very rich landowner, blessed with a large family of seven sons and three daughters. He had an immense ranch: 7,000 sheep, 3,000 camels, 500 yoke of oxen, 500 female donkeys, and a huge household of staff. To show how he feared God and shunned evil and how he loved his children, the account says his children enjoyed partying at each other's houses and after each time of feasting, Job had a habit of offering sacrifices to God just in case any one of them had cursed[1] God in their hearts. He did this regularly to put them right with God.

The stage is set, but then the narrative tells of a scene behind that scene. It is set in the heavens. It was a great gathering of the sons of God coming to present themselves to God. And Satan showed up. Satan is a fallen angel who was initially a guardian cherub, guardian of the earth, called Lucifer. The Lord asked him where he'd come from, and his answer was that he had been "going to and fro on the earth, and . . . walking back and forth on it."

---

1   Literally "blessed," but in an evil sense, amounting to mockery and hypocrisy. This occurs a number of times in Job. The NKJV, Cambridge University Press Bible reference for Job 1:5, 1:11, 2:5, and 2:9 states: literally blessed but in an evil sense. This difficult concept is clarified by Isaiah 29:13—"Therefore the Lord said: 'Inasmuch as these people draw near with their mouths and honor Me with their lips, but have removed their hearts far from Me, and their fear toward Me is taught by the commandment of men.'" It is quoted by Jesus in Mark 7:6. "Well did Isaiah prophesy of you hypocrites, as it is written: 'This people honors Me with *their* lips, but their heart is far from Me.'" Job's concern for his children here is that they may have fallen into this very trap.

The Lord also asked Satan if he had considered his servant Job, a man like no other, who was "a blameless and upright man, one who fears God and shuns evil" (Job 1:8).

In asking this question—"Have you considered My servant Job?"—God put a spotlight on Job. It is the first of a number of spotlights we will look at in this whole account. All the characters in this story—Job, God, Satan, and the three friends—are highlighted for special consideration.

The enemy, Satan, had certainly considered Job, but couldn't touch him because of God's hedge all about him. So, he answered God:

> "Does Job fear God for nothing? Have You not made a hedge around him, around his household, and around all that he has on every side? You have blessed the work of his hands, and his possessions have increased in the land. But now, stretch out **Your hand** and touch all he has, and he will surely curse You to Your face!"
>
> And the Lord said to Satan, "Behold, all that he has *is* in your power [literally hand]; only do not lay a hand on his *person*."

So Satan went out from the presence of the Lord. (Job 1:9–12, emphasis added)

Satan urged God to stretch out *his hand* and touch all he had detrimentally, convinced that it would result in Job cursing God to his face. The Lord seemed to concur and go along with Satan's suggestion. He did not agree to stretch out his own hand to touch Job, but he allowed, even commissioned, Satan to have all that Job owned in his, Satan's, power—literally in his hand. It seemed to amount to the same thing, whether by God's hand or Satan's, which was the utter destruction of all that was Job's.

It is vital to understand the nature of God's goodness by the works of his hand. The Bible is full of references to the hand and works of God. For example:

> Isaiah 41:10—"Fear not, for I *am* with you; be not dismayed, for I *am* your God. I will strengthen you, yes, I will help you, I will uphold you with My righteous right hand."

> Psalm 60:5—"That Your beloved may be delivered, save *with* Your right hand, and hear me."

> Psalm 111:7—"The works of His hands *are* verity and justice."

> Psalm 138:7—"Though I walk in the midst of trouble, You will revive me; You will stretch out Your hand against the wrath of my enemies and Your right hand will save me."

God's right hand is good and righteous, not wrong and evil. King David, who was described as a man after God's own heart, wrote many examples of this in the Psalms.

King David said, in 2 Samuel 24:14, during one great trial in his life, "Please let me fall into the Hand of the Lord, for

His mercies *are* great; but do not let me fall into the hand of man."

So, in this first heavenly convocation in Job, in the scene behind the scene, God turned the spotlight on Job for Satan, and gave permission that everything of Job's be in Satan's hands, but that he was not to lay a hand on Job's person.

What ensued was absolute devastation and catastrophic tragedy. Satan went out and did his work to the full extent of his fallen nature's purpose on earth. By his hand, it was as in times of war and disaster. In a single day, Job lost his entire livestock and his beloved sons and daughters. The news of each loss came in a staccato of machine-gun-like robbery and slaughter. It was the utter destruction of all that was Job's.

> Then Job arose, tore his robe, and shaved his head; and he fell to the ground and worshiped. And he said:
>
> "Naked I came from my mother's womb, and naked shall I return there. The Lord gave, and the Lord has taken away; Blessed be the name of the Lord."
>
> In all this Job did not sin nor charge God with wrong. (Job 1:20–22)

SCENE 2

Adam's Seed in the Best of Men

For who in the heavens can be compared to the Lord? *Who* among the sons of the mighty can be likened to the Lord? God is greatly to be feared in the assembly of the saints, and to be held in reverence by all *those* around Him. O Lord God of hosts, who *is* mighty like You, O Lord? Your faithfulness also surrounds You. (Ps 89:6–8)

I will turn My hand against you, and thoroughly purge away your dross, and take away all your alloy. (Isa 1:25)

Later, there was another gathering of the sons of God in the scene behind the scene, and again Satan turned up from his earth wanderings. The Lord asked him a second time if he had considered the "one" he called "My servant Job," presenting him still as "none like him on the earth, a blameless and upright man, one who fears God and shuns evil? And still he holds fast to his integrity, although you incited Me against him, to destroy him without cause" (Job 2:3).

In the end, the cause emerges and is seen. The seed of Adam's sin will cause every one of God's human beings, originally made in his image, to be remade in Satan's image, and thereby be subject to the king over all who are proud; in other words, final independence from God.

It was then that Satan, the accuser, played his best curse card:

7

"Skin for skin! Yes, all that a man has he will give for his life. But stretch out Your hand now, and touch his bone and his flesh, and he will surely curse You to Your face!"

And the Lord said to Satan, "Behold, he *is* in your hand, but spare his life." (Job 2:4–6)

Again, Satan wanted God to stretch out his hand to destroy Job, and again God said, in effect, my hand will not touch him for evil, but I give permission for him to be in *your* hand, you accuser and destroyer.

What is God getting at, allowing one made in his image to be handed over into the hands of one so cruel, evil, and bent on destruction?

A flashback to the Garden of Eden is needed here, full of the richest provision, with God, Adam, and Eve. God said, in effect, you are my friends, made in my image. Everything is yours, except the tree of the knowledge of good and evil. It represents one who knew only good, but came to know evil too. Don't touch it, or you will lose my image and become like it. It represents Satan. Adam and Eve were already made in the image of God.

> Then God said, "Let Us make man in Our image, according to Our likeness; let them have dominion over the fish of the sea, over the birds of the air, and over the cattle, over all the earth and over every creeping thing that creeps on the earth." So, God created man in His *own* image; in the image of God

He created him; male and female He created them. (Gen 1:26–27).

To eat of that tree was to die out of the image of God and to be remade into the image of Lucifer become Satan! That is the god Satan referred to: "For God knows that in the day you eat of it your eyes will be opened, and you will be like God, knowing good and evil" (Gen 3:5). The hard testing was to separate Job—and us all—from this legacy of the seed of Adam and Eve's sin.

Along the way, Job asked the question that coruscates with hints of the heart of the matter: "*Am* I a sea or a sea serpent [like Leviathan, the dragon], that You set a guard over me?" (Job 7:12). In other words, has Job become a sea (in heaven there will be no sea) or a sea serpent like Leviathan, the dragon who is so fierce and independent from God that God has to set a guard over him? Satan was originally Lucifer, made by God, a guardian cherub over the earth. The description of the king of Tyre in Ezekiel 28 is really a picture of Lucifer's former station, fall, and destiny.

> Moreover, the Word of the Lord came to me, saying, "Son of man, take up a lamentation for the king of Tyre, and say to him, 'Thus says the Lord God:
>
> "You *were* the seal of perfection, full of wisdom and perfect in beauty. You were in Eden, the garden of God; every precious stone *was* your covering: sardius, topaz, and diamond, beryl, onyx, and jasper, sapphire, turquoise, and emerald with gold.

The workmanship of your timbrels and pipes was prepared for you on the day you were created.

"You *were* the anointed cherub who covers; I established you; you were on the holy mountain of God; you walked back and forth in the midst of fiery stones. You *were* perfect in your ways from the day you were created, till iniquity was found in you.

"By the abundance of your trading you became filled with violence within, and you sinned; therefore I cast you as a profane thing out of the mountain of God; and I destroyed you, O covering cherub, from the midst of the fiery stones.

"Your heart was lifted up [proud] because of your beauty; you corrupted your wisdom for the sake of your splendor; I cast you to the ground, I laid you before kings, that they might gaze at you.

"You defiled your sanctuaries by the multitude of your iniquities, by the iniquity of your trading; therefore I brought fire from your midst; it devoured you, and I turned you to ashes upon the earth in the sight of all who saw you. All who knew you among the peoples are astonished at you; you have become a horror, and *shall* be no more forever.""" (Ezek 28:11–19)

Isaiah 14 also describes Lucifer's place in heaven, ambition, and fall, which we will look at later.

The serpent's temptation of Adam and Eve gives a clear understanding of his purpose for them:

Now the serpent was more cunning than any beast of the field which the Lord God had made. And he said to the woman, "Has God indeed said, 'You shall not eat of every tree of the garden'?"

And the woman said to the serpent, "We may eat the fruit of the trees of the garden; but the fruit of the tree which is in the midst of the garden, God has said, 'You shall not eat it, nor shall you touch it lest you die.'"

Then the serpent said to the woman, "You will not surely die. For God knows that in the day you eat of it your eyes will be opened, and you will be like God, knowing good and evil." (Gen 3:1–5)

Here the serpent called God a liar! God said, "You will die." The serpent said, "You will not die!" The serpent seemed to be telling the truth. Adam and Eve appeared not to die.

What died immediately when they disobeyed God and concurred with the serpent was their spirits, by which they fellowshipped and had intimacy with God. They had been made like God with all his attributes: truth, life, light, love, joy, peace, kindness, goodness, faithfulness, gentleness, and self-control. They were God-conscious and reflected His nature. When they touched and ate the fruit of the tree of the knowledge of good and evil, they immediately became self-conscious and self-focused and were ashamed of their nakedness. Their disobedience to God was self-evident and they hid from him.

Now they were sidetracked. This new track gave them the heritage of the one who was represented by the tree of the knowledge of good and evil. Having known and been like God and his goodness, they would now "know" the serpent's ways, his craftiness, rebellion, and all his attributes, which are opposite to God's: lies, hypocrisy, robbery, death, darkness, hatred, murder, war, disease, cruelty, evil, unfaithfulness, and pride; in fact, all the fruits of the flesh would be in them, and they would be like him.

They lost their friendship with God and also the dominion that he had given them over all the creatures that He had made. The serpent usurped their place of dominion. From being a guardian cherub of the earth, he became the god of this world.

God had to drive Adam and Eve out of the Garden of Eden so they would not eat of the tree of life in its midst while being in their disobedient, altered condition. Because of that, they would live forever in their rebellious state. The legacy of the seed of Adam and Eve's sin resulted in independence from God, being cut off from him in his perfection, and all that he is.

This fallen legacy was even in Job, the best of men. It ultimately leads away from intimacy and trust with God. It marks humankind out for separation from God. The heat of a furnace eventually causes dross to come running out of precious metal. The refining process is for separation, the pure from the impure.

Job's person was now the object of Satan's attack. Having been the recipient of God's blessings, he was now loaded with curses. The enemy struck him with painful boils from head to toe. As Job sat in the ashes of his broken life, his wife, the one closest to him, with whom he was one flesh, said: "Do you still hold fast to your integrity? Curse God and die!" (Job 2:9). Here was a sword in his heart from the one who was obviously heartbroken and embittered herself through the loss of their children, and everything that made up their former life together. "Curse," in his wife's words, was again, literally, "bless," but in an evil sense. This was the beginning of an abysmal stirring. It would bring up things that were so deeply buried in Job he was unaware of their occult presence.

After this, three of Job's friends—Eliphaz the Temanite, Bildad the Shuhite, and Zophar the Naamathite—hearing of Job's sorrows, determined to come together to comfort him. They were so profoundly moved by his sorrows and changed appearance that they wept and joined him in his mourning. They tore their robes, sprinkled dust on their heads, and sat with him on the ground. So great was Job's grief that they sat with him for seven days and seven nights without even saying one word.

Most of us would probably find it difficult, while visiting a suffering friend, to remain silent for seven minutes, not to mention seven days. And while we may plead vast differences in culture, still it is obvious these friends of Job were extraordinary in their concern for their friend. The week he had endured, heavy with heartbreak, was like the moments before another volcanic eruption. "After this, Job opened his mouth and cursed the day of his *birth*. And Job spoke, and said: 'May the day perish on which I was born'" (Job 3:1–3). The first thing he did at this juncture was to roundly curse—not God, but the day of his birth. He even called upon those "who curse the day" and are "ready to arouse Leviathan" (Job 3:8).

This was calling upon witches and warlocks and those who are ready to rouse the devil! In a long soliloquy, Job continued to wish he had never been born, or at least that he had been stillborn, or died soon after birth. He says:

> "Why is light given to him who is in misery, and life to the bitter of soul, who long for death, but it does not *come* ... *why is light given* to a man whose way is hidden and whom God has hedged in?" (Job 3:20–23)

Now that Job's body and soul were so squeezed, his only recourse was to wish and long for a way out. The pressure caused him to curse himself, he who was made in the image of God. He who loved God, and according to God, was a man like no other in this. Now for him there was no ease, quiet, or rest. Trouble had truly come, and was prolonged. From chapter 4 to chapter 25, beginning with Eliphaz, the three friends tried to address Job in this place of despair and utter anguish. So began a terrible miasma, arising at first out of Job's friends' attempts to advise and mediate between him and God. Not having a true grasp of Job or God, it could only end in confusion and bad feeling all around. It became a place where friends didn't get it and turned.

CHAPTER 2

Speaking Right of God—
Speaking Wrong of God

When Friends Don't Get It and Turn

ELIPHAZ

Eliphaz set the tone with his confusing, contradictory first speech. He cautiously began by recalling Job's life of counsel and encouragement of others, but very quickly did a natural summing up in his own eyes of the root of the problem. Although, in Job 4:6–9, Eliphaz says:

> *Is* not your reverence your confidence? And the integrity of your ways your hope?

> "Remember now, who *ever* perished being innocent? Or where were the upright *ever* cut off? Even as I have seen, those who plow iniquity and sow trouble reap the same. By the blast of God

they perish, and by the breath of his anger they are consumed."

But when Eliphaz disclosed that a spirit had secretly revealed some things to him in a night visitation, it became clear his counsel was muddied by a lying spirit of confusion. So, truth and error were mixed in his exhortation, leaving Job more wounded and aware he was a target, and he states, "the arrows of the Almighty *are* within me" (Job 6:4). He cried: "To him who is afflicted, kindness *should be shown* by his friend, even though he forsakes the fear of the Almighty" (Job 6:14).

Eliphaz had actually asked, "*Is* not your reverence your confidence? And the integrity of your ways your hope?" (Job 4:6). He also used the words "innocent" and "upright" in relation to Job (4:7). He said, in effect, he himself would appeal to God (Job 5:8).

Was he thinking that Job's own reverence, integrity, innocence, and uprightness would be enough to answer, when the night-spirit guide said, "Can a mortal be more righteous than God?" (Job 4:17). Or could it be said that a mortal, with his own reverence, can satisfy God's requirement of holiness, even one as upright as Job?

Eliphaz also said, "Behold, happy *is* the man whom God corrects; therefore do not despise the chastening of the Almighty" (Job 5:17). Convinced there was some sin in Job that needed attention, Eliphaz encouraged Job to accept God's chastening. This had the effect of driving Job to distraction because of his own conviction that he had no hidden sin.

Remember God's own testimony of Job: "Have you considered My servant Job, that *there* is none like him on the earth, a blameless and upright man, one who fears God and shuns evil?" (Job 1:8).

Eliphaz's following two speeches spiralled down, accusing his friend of folly, iniquity, and turning his spirit against God. In Job 15:14–15, he said:

> "What *is* man, that he could be pure? And *he who is* born of a woman, that he could be righteous? If *God* puts no trust in his saints, and the heavens are not pure in his sight, how much less man, *who* is abominable and filthy, who drinks iniquity like water?"

In chapter 22, angry at Job because he refused the friends' counsel, Eliphaz poured out a lying diatribe of false accusations against Job. He concluded condescendingly by saying: "Now acquaint yourself with Him and be at peace; thereby good will come to you" (Job 22:21). He also said, "He [God] will *even* deliver one who is not innocent; yes, he will be delivered by the purity of your hands" (Job 22:30). In other words, when you humble yourself, God will save you, and you will be able to partner with God and save others who are not innocent.

BILDAD

In chapter 7, Job spoke to God in the anguish of his spirit and said God was scaring him, terrifying him with dreams and visions. He vividly painted a picture of his own life in this trial as a time of hard service, having been allotted months of futility, tossing and turning at night, and with his flesh caked with worms and dust and cracking with fresh outbreaks. Again, he pleaded with God for an end to his loathed life, saying he chose "strangling *and* death" rather than his body. He cried out:

> Have I sinned? What have I done to you, O watcher of men? Why have You set me as Your target, so that I am a burden to myself? Why then do you not pardon my transgression, and take away my iniquity? For now I will lie down in the dust, and you will seek me diligently, but I *will* no longer *be.*" (Job 7:20–21)

There are some good questions and comments here. To this, Bildad began his response to Job. But, as with Eliphaz, there is rebuke for Job from Bildad for speaking "hot air" and rhetorical questions.

> Does God subvert judgment? Or does the Almighty pervert justice? If your sons have sinned against Him, He has cast them away for their transgression. If you would earnestly seek God and make your supplication to the Almighty (Job 8:3–5)

As if Job had not been doing just that! However, Bildad ended his first speech on an encouraging note:

> Behold, God will not cast away the blameless, nor will He uphold the evildoers. He will yet fill your mouth with laughing, and your lips with rejoicing. Those who hate you will be clothed with shame, and the dwelling place of the wicked will come to nothing. (Job 8:20–22)

Job actually agreed with Bildad, and he also acknowledged:

> Truly I know *it is* so, but how can a man be righteous before God?[2] If one wished to contend with Him, He could not answer Him one time out of a thousand. *God is* wise in heart and mighty in strength. Who has hardened *himself* against Him and prospered?" (Job 9:2–4)

In chapter 9, Job continued describing God's majesty in his doings, and in 9:14 he said: "How can I then answer Him, *and* choose my words *to reason* with Him? For though I were righteous, I could not answer Him; I would beg mercy of my Judge" (Job 9:14–15). But Job went on to say that even if he called and God answered him, he would not believe God was listening to his voice, because he was experiencing wounds and crushing from God, and bitterness. In Job 9:20–22 and 24, Job said:

---

2   Which is different from, "Can a man be more righteous than God?"—the question from Eliphaz's night visitor.

"Though I were righteous, my own mouth would condemn me; though I *were* blameless, it would prove me perverse.

"I am blameless, yet I do not know myself; I despise my life. It *is* all one *thing*; therefore I say, 'He destroys the blameless and the wicked.' ... The earth is given into the **hand of the wicked**. He covers the faces of its judges. If it is not *He*, who else could it be?" (emphasis added).

Further, Job asked a crucial question:

I will say to God, "Do not condemn me; **show me why You contend with me**. *Does it* seem good to You that You should oppress, that You should despise the work of Your hands [me], and smile on the counsel of the wicked [the accuser]? Do You have eyes of flesh?[3] Or do You see as man sees? *Are* Your days like the days of a mortal man? *Are* Your years like the days of a mighty man, that You should seek for my iniquity and search out my sin, although You know that I am not wicked, and *there is* no one who can deliver from Your hand?" (Job 10:2–7, emphasis added)

These three Statements from Job are very important:

1. "I am blameless, yet I do not know myself" (Job 9:21).

2. "I will say to God, 'Do not condemn me; show me why You contend with me'" (Job 10:2).

---

3   Of course, he doesn't know that Jesus the Son of God is coming, who will have eyes of flesh.

3. "You should seek for my iniquity and search out my sin, although you know that I am not wicked" (Job 10:6–7).

Over and over, Job wept over this enigma. Job claimed himself blameless, but also owned he didn't know himself. He purposed to ask God not to condemn him, but to show him why God contended with him. And in frustration, Job said, "You seek for my iniquity and … sin, although you **know that I am not wicked**" (Job 10:6–7, emphasis added)! This is worth repeating! There is something else, something deep—a missing piece of the puzzle—that needs unearthing.

Could it be, as Job said, "the earth is given into the hands of the wicked" for this as yet unseen purpose of the Almighty? We recall in Job 1:12, God said to the wicked one, "Behold, all that he has *is* in your power"—it literally is in your hands.

Job kept referring to God. The friends muddled along, seeming to represent God, but coming from their own judgment of outer appearances.

Bildad summed it up in Job 18. In effect, he said Job was trapped in darkness and despair; his own counsels had cast him down; he was ensnared, terrified, destroyed inwardly and outwardly; to be paraded before the king of terrors; driven from light to darkness; not renowned; uprooted from his tent; without son or posterity or anyone. Therefore, he had to be in the place of those who do not know God.

How heartbreaking this was for Job, who knew he had lived his life serving God in every way he knew possible. In chapter 31, Job gave an honest-before-God account of his life and doings to refute Bildad's and his other friends' hostile attacks on his veracity. The whole focus of his life, his lodestar, was to know, love, and serve God.

After Bildad's scathing comments in chapter 18, Job cried:

> "How long will you torment my soul, and break me in pieces with words? These ten times you have reproached me; you are not ashamed *that* you have wronged me. And if indeed I have erred, my error remains with me. If indeed you exalt *yourselves* against me, and plead my disgrace against me, know then that God has wronged me, and has surrounded me with His net." (Job 19:1–6)

Job stated plainly, you have wronged me! And God has wronged me! He had said previously his friends were "forgers of lies . . . worthless physicians" (Job 13:4), and their silence would be their wisdom (Job 13:5). He said also they were "miserable comforters" Job 16:2). No wonder they were upset at Job. Out of his pitiable condition, he pleaded for pity (Job 19:1), and entered into his most sublime statement of faith:

> "Oh, that my words were written! Oh, that they were inscribed in a book! That they were engraved on a rock with an iron pen and lead, forever! **For I know that my Redeemer lives**, and He shall stand at last on the earth; and after my skin is destroyed,

this *I know*, that in my flesh I shall see God, whom
I shall see for myself, and my eyes shall behold, and
not another." (Job 19:23–27, emphasis added)

Astonishing! This is sheer faith.

Then Job warned his friends that they should be afraid of the sword, punishment, and judgment. Surveying violence and injustice in the world, Job said, "So, the grave *consumes those who* have sinned. The womb *should* forget him, the worm *should* feed sweetly on him" (Job 24:19–20). In other words, there should be judgment on the wicked. Little did he know there is a worm intent on doing just that: feeding sweetly on all the descendants of Adam who have inherited the seed of Adam's sin.

In a final, short word in Job 25:4, Bildad again had an odd mixture of thoughts of God, and repeated the words already put forth, namely, "How then can man be righteous before God?"

This penultimate question of Bildad's reaches forward prophetically to the ultimate redemptive purpose of God: "Or how he can be pure *who is* born of a woman? If even the moon does not shine, and the stars are not pure in His sight, how much less man, *who is* a maggot, and a son of man, *who is* a worm?" (Job 25:4–5).

Man was made in the image of God. Independence from God, via his God- given freedom, set man on a maggoty course. Here is a puzzling prophetic passage. It hints of the Son of God, who became a son of man, "who knew no sin *to be* sin for us, that we might become the righteousness of God in Him" (2 Cor 5:21). And all this by the set purpose of God.

But man born of Adam's line, and born of a woman, cannot be pure before God. Bildad was saying if there are those in the heavenly places who cannot be pure in God's sight, then certainly a son of man, who is a maggot or a worm, cannot be pure.

David's Psalm 22 is full of prophetic references to the Messiah. It begins with the enigmatic words Jesus cried from the cross, "My God, My God, why have you forsaken me?" It goes on,

> *Why are You so* far from helping Me, *and from* the words of My groaning? O My God, I cry in the daytime, but You do not hear; and in the night season, and am not silent.
>
> But You *are* holy, enthroned on the praises of Israel. Our fathers trusted in You; they trusted, and You delivered them. They cried to You, and were delivered; they trusted in You and were not ashamed.
>
> But I *am* a worm, and no man; a reproach of men, and despised by the people. All those who see Me ridicule Me; they shoot out the lip, they shake the head, *saying* "He trusted in the Lord, let Him rescue Him; let Him deliver Him, since He delights in Him!" (Ps 22:1–8)

David's psalm foreshadowed the suffering servant Messiah, who would humble himself to such a level as to call himself, prophetically, a *worm*, and no man. This, in order to rescue the human race by taking their sin on himself and dying in their place. Later, we will look again at Messianic prophecies delineating the Messiah's birth, life, death by crucifixion, and resurrection.

> "For He [God, the Father] made Him [God the Son] who knew no sin *to be* sin for us, that we might become the righteousness of God in Him." (2 Cor 5:21)

This points to the reason for God's probe in Job. Even the best of men need redemption. There was and is only one best man whom death could not hold. He had to descend to become a son of man and "a worm" to redeem humankind.

ZOPHAR

Zophar heard Job's sublime, agonized declaration of faith and *didn't hear*. In a most venomous, angry response, he spoke "for God," but didn't! His virulent attack on Job used words such as wicked, haughtiness, hypocrite, and evil. His lying accusations dreamed up all manner of false scenarios and evil consequences in Job's life. His litany of lies were curses, which he summed up by saying, "This *is* the portion from God for a wicked man, the heritage appointed to him by God" (Job 20:29)! Even earlier, Job 11:5, Zophar blasted, "But oh, that God would speak, and open His lips against you."

Job answered him by comparing his own life with the lives of those wicked people who seem to get off scotfree. From Job 21: "Look at me and be astonished" (v. 5), and, "Why do the wicked live and become old, yes and mighty in power?" (v.7).

> "They spend their days in wealth, and in a moment go down to the grave. Yet they say to God, 'depart from us, for we do not desire the knowledge of Your ways. Who is the Almighty, that we should serve Him?'" (vv. 13–15).

Job said to the three friends:

> "Look, I know your thoughts and the schemes *with which* you would wrong me. For you say, 'Where is the house of the prince [Job]? And where *is* the tent, the dwelling place of the wicked?' . . . How then can you comfort me with empty words, since falsehood [faithlessness] remains in your answers?" (Job 21:27–28; 34).

The three friends, intent from the outset on comforting their suffering friend Job, in responding to his bitterness, failed to see what was really at the root. They must have believed they were being pragmatic, but they were widely off target in sizing up his situation.

CHAPTER 3

The Crucible for Silver
and the Furnace for Gold

It is important to look more closely at this first spotlight on Job to see exactly what rose to the surface of his life under such close scrutiny and agonizing pain of the protracted trial. Basically, three things emerged:

1. He cursed himself;
2. He shook his fist at God, saying God denied him justice; and,
3. He cursed others by calling them fools.

1. He can clearly be seen cursing himself, as was discussed earlier, when in Job 3:3 he said, "May the day perish on which I was born," and in 3:11, "Why did I not die at birth? *Why* did I *not* perish when I came from the womb?"

He was even calling upon agents of darkness to curse the day of his birth. He, who was made in the image of God, wished rather for death than the misery and bitterness of this trial. Later on, Elihu, the fourth friend, had light to shed relating to this. In Job 36:21 NIV, he said, "Beware of turning to evil, which you seem to prefer to affliction."

2. In much of his discourse, Job spoke what was right about God. But he came to the place of accusing God of denying him justice! He states, "Know then that God has wronged me" (Job 19:6).

> "*As* God lives, *who* has taken away my justice and the Almighty, *who* has made my soul bitter, as long as breath *is* in me, and the breath of God in my nostrils, my lips will not speak wickedness, nor my tongue utter deceit. Far be it from me that I should say you are right; till I die I will not put away my integrity from me. My righteousness I hold fast and will not let it go; my heart shall not reproach *me* as long as I live." (Job 27:1–6)

He knew he was right. He believed he was right—more right—than God! But he didn't reckon with the seed of Adam's sin in him. He was not a wicked man, but within Job, the best of men, was this ticking time bomb. It only awaited the right circumstances, a time of incubation, as it were, to manifest something of the accuser. Everything of the accuser is rebellion against God. And so, God brought about those circumstances that would cause the incubation: the heat of the furnace. Without this seed surfacing, it would remain within, and ultimately be enough evidence that he was a subject to the "king over all that are proud" (Job 41:34 NIV).

Job's own righteousness was not enough to deliver him from this. Job himself said, "Who can bring a clean *thing* out of an unclean? No one!" (Job 14:4), and in 14:7, "there is hope for a tree, if it is cut down, that it will sprout again," but in verse 10, "man dies and is laid away; indeed he breathes his last and where *is* he?" In Job 14:14, he said, "If a man dies, shall he live *again*? All the days of my hard service I will wait, till my change comes."

But where now was Job's hope if indeed God denied him justice?

3. In the final chapters of his discourse and defence, Job said to his friends,

> "I will teach you about the hand of God; what *is* with the Almighty I will not conceal. Surely all of you have seen *it*; why then do you behave with complete nonsense?" (Job 27:11–12)

Job spoke on the portion of the wicked. And then he taught about wisdom and where it can be found, culminating in the Scriptural treasure: "And to man He said, 'Behold the fear of the Lord, that *is* wisdom, and to depart from evil *is* understanding'" (Job 28:28). Sublime!

But then, Job came down with a mighty error. In Job 30:8, he referenced a group of men who had mocked him and referred to them as sons of fools: "*They were* sons of fools, yes, sons of vile men; they were scourged from the land." Job must have been sorely tried by these men to denigrate and curse them in this way. In Matthew 5:22, Jesus Christ said:

> But I say to you that whoever is angry with his brother without a cause shall be in danger of the judgment. And whoever says to his brother 'Raca!' [literally in Aramaic: Empty head] shall be in danger of the council. But whoever says, 'You fool!' shall be in danger of hell fire.

To be translated out of this present darkness, even under the greatest provocation, we need to go the way of the Redeemer, who said:

> [L]ove your enemies, bless those who curse you, do good to those who hate you, and pray for those who spitefully use you and persecute you, **that you may be sons of your Father in heaven**; for He makes His sun rise on the evil and on the good, and sends rain on the just and the unjust. [. . .] Therefore you shall be perfect, just as your Father in heaven is perfect. (Matthew 5:44–45; 48, emphasis added).

To live again, from our deathly heritage, there needs to be a death of all the old things and ways. Simply reiterated, our righteousness is not enough. Few people live such exemplary lives as Job's, yet his righteousness was not enough.

But we must look more closely at his righteous life, recorded in his final defence in Job 30 and 31. His precursor was:

> "I cry out to You, but You do not answer me; I stand up, and You regard me. *But* You have become cruel to me; with the strength of Your hand You oppose me. You lift me up to the wind and cause

me to ride *on it*[4]; You spoil my success. For I know *that* You will bring me *to* death, and to the house appointed for all the living.

"Surely, He would not stretch out *His* hand against a heap of ruins, if they cry out when He destroys *it*." (Job 30:20–24)

---

4   In other words, "you blow me all over the place."

In Job 30:25 and then in 31:1–40, Job began to list all the good things in his life that should give the Lord pause before destroying him. He wept for those in trouble and his soul was "grieved for the poor." In recounting this, he thought of his own poor state now and said, "My harp is *tuned* to mourning, and my flute to the voice of those who weep" (Job 30:31).

He went on to say that he had made a covenant with his eyes not to look lustfully at a young woman because wasn't that "destruction for the wicked, and disaster for the workers of iniquity? Does He [God] not see my ways and count all my steps?" (Job 31:3–4).

God sees it all, and knows and deals with sin. Because of this, Job purposed in his heart to refuse to despise the cause of his servants when they had a complaint against him (Job 31:13). He supplied the desire of the poor, needy, and widow, and generously shared his food and home with the orphan (vv. 16–18). He clothed the poor and was blessed for doing it (v. 20). He did not set his heart on his gold or rejoice in his great wealth (vv. 24–25), neither did he idolatrously worship the sun and moon (v. 26). He said he did not rejoice at the destruction of his enemies (v. 29), or allow his mouth to sin by cursing the one who hated him (v. 30). He had shared his food with all, so men of his household said, "Who is there that has not been satisfied with his meat?" (Job 31:31). All travellers were welcomed into his house (v. 32). He was even bold enough to say he did not hide his transgressions as Adam or as men do (v. 33).

He wanted someone to hear him. He longed that the Almighty would answer him, and even that his "Prosecutor [literally, the accuser] had written a book" (Job 31:35).

Again, Job wished it was all written down in a book.

He concluded by declaring a curse on himself if he had even wronged his land by eating its fruit without investment, or "caused its owners to lose their lives" (Job 31:39); in other words, killed someone for their land that was rented from him. Here, "The words of Job are ended" (Job 31:40).

The three friends, with all their exasperation and arguments, had failed to convince and convict Job, had failed in fact to put their finger on the real problem.

CHAPTER 4

Enter Elihu, God's Representative

> For the Lord *is* righteous, He loves righteousness;
> His countenance beholds the upright. (Ps 11:7)

> Do not enter into judgment with Your servant, for
> in Your sight no one living is righteous. (Ps 143:2)

> But we are all like an unclean *thing*, and all our
> righteousnesses *are* like filthy rags; we all fade as a
> leaf, and our iniquities, like the wind, have taken us
> away. (Isa 64:6)

Enter Elihu, God's representative. In Job 32–36, he stood
up to address the "root." He recognized the heart of the
problem, despite being younger than Eliphaz, Bildad, and
Zophar. His name means "My God is he"—or God himself.
This is startling, considering the role he was called upon
to play in the life of Job. He had an interesting mixture of
patience, humility, and boldness. He had waited for the
others to completely have their say. He listened intently to

their lines of argument, finding them ineffectual. He also paid attention to Job's reasoning and claims. He affirmed clearly that he was both angry with Job for justifying himself rather than God, and with the friends because "they had found no answer, and *yet* had condemned Job" (Job 32:3). Later, he said that he wanted to justify Job and to see him cleared (Job 33:32).

Here is a specially appointed and anointed person to represent God—and Job—by seeing clearly and telling the truth. His counsel contains elements of comfort, help, and guidance into the truth that makes us free. It was infused with supernatural comprehension and ontological briefing.

> "But *there* is a spirit in man and the breath of the Almighty gives him understanding. Great men are not *always* wise, nor do the aged *always* understand justice.

> "Therefore, I say, 'Listen to me, I will also declare my opinion'." (Job 32:8)

Elihu said he was bursting to speak, but out of fear of the Lord would not flatter anyone or show partiality. And so, he began, as Job's "spokesman before God" (Job 33:6), though he affirmed he was also "formed out of clay" so that no fear of him should terrify Job. He did, however, cut straight to the quick by quoting Job's claim to purity and innocence:

> "Surely you have spoken in my hearing, and I have heard the sounds of *your* words *saying*, 'I *am* pure, without transgression; I *am* innocent, and

> *there is* no iniquity in me. Yet He finds occasions
> against me; He counts me as His enemy; He puts
> my feet in the stocks, He watches all my paths.'"
> (Job 33:8–11)

Elihu squarely answered this claim:

> "Look, *in* this you are not righteous. I will answer
> you, for God is greater than man. Why do you
> contend with Him? For He does not give an
> accounting of any of His Words. For God may
> speak in one way or another, *yet man* does not per-
> ceive it" (Job 33:12–14).

Then Elihu listed some of the ways God may speak. It could
be through dreams or visions; or chastening on a bed of
pain. His purpose is to turn man from wrong deeds and
pride, and to deliver them from going down to the pit and
judgment. God desires people to have a mediator, who will
turn them back from death and judgment, who will enable
them to see God's uprightness and grace, who will find for
them a ransom or atonement so that they can be restored to
God's righteousness. In fact, Elihu wanted Job to see God
is indeed involved in the process of mirroring for mankind
how things really are, and how God really is, to the end that
man's soul can be brought back and redeemed.

King David wrote in Psalm 36:9: "With You *is* the fountain
of life; in Your light we see light."

With great perspicacity, Elihu quoted Job and answered
him on behalf of God:

"For Job has said, 'I am righteous, but God has taken away my justice; should I lie concerning my right? My wound *is* incurable, *though I am* without transgression.' What man *is* like Job . . . ? For he has said, 'It profits a man nothing that he should delight in God.'

"Therefore, listen to me you men of understanding. Far be it from God *to do* wickedness, and *from* the Almighty to *commit* iniquity. For He repays man *according to* his work, and makes man find a reward according to *his* way. Surely God will never do wickedly, nor will the Almighty pervert justice. Who gave Him charge over the earth? . . . If He should set His heart on it, *if* He should gather to Himself His Spirit and His breath, all flesh would perish together, and man would return to the dust.

"If *you have* understanding, hear this; listen to the sound of my words: Should one who hates justice govern? Will you condemn *Him who* is most just?" (Job 34:5–7;9–17).

He said God sees and knows everything:

"has *anyone* said to God, 'I have borne *chastening*; I will offend no more; teach me *what* I do not see; if I have done iniquity, I will do no more'? Should He repay *it* according **to your terms**, *just* because you disavow it? You must choose and not I" (Job 34:31–33, emphasis added).

Perhaps Job came close when he said, "I do not know myself" (Job 9:21), and "Make me know my transgression and my sin" (Job 13:23)?

Perhaps this was why Elihu had said, "Speak, for I desire to justify you. If not, listen to me; hold your peace, and I will teach you wisdom" (Job 33:32–33)?

But how can anyone be taught wisdom who thinks their "righteousness is more than God's" (Job 35:2), and who "multiplies words without knowledge" (Job 35:16)— without full knowledge, that is.

Elihu was preparing Job for the coming approach of God; this was truly an advent of that encounter Job had longed for. But it was very difficult as Elihu boldly stated, on the one hand he would "ascribe righteousness to [his] Maker," and on the other hand, "one who is perfect in knowledge *is* with you" (Job 36:3–4).

Was he saying that God was already present without Job recognizing it? He spoke personally and intimately about God, his strength, his understanding, and his being unwilling to despise anyone. His teaching Job wisdom was thorough, giving him a rounded picture of God's justice to the oppressed; his eyes on the righteous to reward and exalt them; his showing them their doings and transgression, and his loving opening of their ears to instruction so that they can turn from iniquity. By obedience they, the righteous, will blossom and flourish again, but dyed-in-the-wool hypocrites were storing up wrath for themselves. Hypocrites are pretenders and manipulators who have no immediate need for God, independent from the very one who gave them breath. This truly is the road to ruin.

Elihu then made it very clear to Job that God desired to bring him out of this terrible distress into a place of great relief and blessing, but something was hindering this desire of God:

> But now you are laden with the judgment due the wicked; judgment and justice have taken hold of you. (Job 36:17 NIV).

> Beware of turning to evil, which you seem to prefer to affliction. (Job 36:21, NIV).

In this fallen world, affliction will come; the only safe place to turn in affliction is to God, in whose "light we see light" (Ps 36:9). In other words, we can only be saved from becoming the darkness in the darkness, when we turn to God who is the light of the world.

> In the beginning was the Word, and the Word was with God, and the Word was God. He was in the beginning with God. All things were made through Him, and without Him nothing was made that was made. In Him was life, and the life was the light of men. And the light shines in the darkness, and the darkness did not comprehend [or overcome] it. (John 1:1–5)

Here Elihu held up a great reminder. He said, *remember*.

"Remember to magnify His work, of which men have sung. Everyone has seen it; man looks on *it* from afar.

"Behold God *is* great, and we do not know Him, nor can the number of His years *be* discovered." (Job 36:24–26).

Almost as if on a time-lapse camera, Elihu then launched into a glorious description of God as Creator, and His creation. He described the water drops and rain; the mystery of cloud coverings which are loaded with water to pour down on the earth and mankind. There is the thunder of God's majesty and His lightning. "God thunders marvelously with His voice; He does great things which we cannot comprehend" (Job 37:5).

A great picture is presented of God orchestrating His snow, ice, and rain; his dealing with man and animals. Then Elihu said, "Listen to this, O Job; stand still and consider the wondrous works of God" (Job 37:14).

And then began a series of questions levelled at Job, begun by Elihu and continued by God himself. For example:

Do you know when God dispatches them, and causes the light of His cloud to shine? Do you know how the clouds are balanced, those wondrous works of Him who is perfect in knowledge? Why are your garments hot, when he quiets the earth by His south *wind*? With Him, have you spread out the skies, strong as a cast metal mirror?

"Teach us what we should say to Him, *for* we can prepare nothing because of the darkness" (Job 37:15–19).

It's as if he said, "We are in the dark, Job, but now get ready; the Almighty God in all His glorious majesty approaches!"

"He comes from the north as golden *splendor*; with God *is* awesome majesty. *As for* the Almighty, we cannot find Him; *He is* excellent in power, *in* judgment and abundant justice; He does not oppress. Therefore men fear Him; He shows no partiality to any *who are* wise of heart." (Job 37:22–24)

Job had ignored all extraneous voices, but now he was faced with untainted truth and relevance; and a response from the Lord that was overwhelming.

CHAPTER 5

The Second Spotlight: On God and His Probe in Job

> We give thanks to You, O God, we give thanks! For your wondrous works declare *that* Your name is near. (Ps 75:1).

> His face was like the sun shining in all its brilliance. (Rev 1:16 NIV).

Who can put a spotlight on God? Obviously, no one! Who can look at the face of God, which is like the sun, shining in all its brilliance?

Yet this was what Job desired—or thought he did—to meet with God. So, the Word Himself reflects the brilliance, and tells the story—paints the picture of the Almighty Creator of the universe in all the effulgence of his power and majesty. The second spotlight, on God, it is obviously a metaphor. It means focus. Focus on God, who he is, and what his hands and voice have created. It is a tour of God's breathtaking creation, with God himself as tour guide. It is like a matchless symphony conducted by God himself:

> what may be known of God is manifest in them [evident among them], for God has shown *it* to them. For since the creation of the world His invisible *attributes* are clearly seen, being understood by the things that are made, *even* His eternal power and Godhead . . . (Rom 1:19–20)

At the threshold of this unveiling of omnipotence,

> [T]he Lord answered Job out of the whirlwind and said:
>
> "Who *is* this who darkens counsel with words without knowledge? Now prepare yourself like a man; I will question you, and you shall answer Me.
>
> "Where were you when I laid the foundations of the earth? Tell *Me*, if you have understanding. Who determined its measurements? Surely you know! Or who stretched the [measuring] line upon it? To what were its foundations fastened? Or who laid its cornerstone, when the morning stars sang together, and all the sons of God shouted for joy?" (Job 38:1–7)

Who did this? Who did that?

> "Or w*ho* shut in the sea with doors, when it burst forth *and* issued from the womb; when I made the clouds its garment, and thick darkness its swaddling

band; when I fixed My limit for it, and set bars and
doors; when I said, 'This far you may come, but no
farther, and here your proud waves must stop!'

"Have you commanded the morning since your
days *began, and* caused the dawn to know its place,
that it might take hold of the ends of the earth, and
the wicked be shaken out of it?"

[. . .]

"Have you entered the springs of the sea? . . . Have
the gates of death been revealed to you? . . . Have
you comprehended the breadth of the earth? . . .

"Where *is* the way *to* the dwelling of light? And
darkness, where *is* its place, that you may take it to
its territory? . . . Do you know *it*, because you were
born then, or *because* the number of your days *is*
great?" (Job 38:8–13; 16–21)

Snow and light and channels for the water; rain and ice and
the heavenly constellations; clouds and lightning; wisdom
of the mind; "the dust hardens in clumps, and the clods
cling together" (Job 38:38).

The kaleidoscope of creation continued and ran on into the
animal kingdom: the lions, ravens, wild mountain goats,
and deer and donkeys and more. Do you know who pro-
vides for them and when they give birth? God continued to
describe the creatures He had made, the strong, the weak,
the wise, the foolish; all the time grilling Job, it seemed,

with a mighty light in His eye, which rang with "Where were you when I made all this?"

After the encompassing commentary on his creation, the Lord weighed in with this question:

> "Shall the one who contends with the Almighty correct *Him*? He who rebukes God, let him answer it."

Then Job answered the Lord and said:

> "Behold I am vile; what shall I answer You? I lay my hand over my mouth. Once I have spoken, but I will not answer; yes, twice, but I will proceed no further." (Job 40:2–5)

Job was certainly getting the picture, but God would not let him off the hook. More probing was needed! The Lord, with laser-like precision, reached the heart of the matter. Again, out of the whirlwind He said:

> "'Now prepare yourself like a man; I will question you and you shall answer Me:
>
> **"Would you indeed annul My judgment? Would you condemn Me that you may be justified?** Have you an arm like God? Or can you thunder with a voice like His? Then adorn yourself *with* majesty and splendor, and array yourself with glory and beauty. Disperse the rage of your wrath; **look on everyone who is proud and humble him**. Look on everyone *who is* proud *and* bring him low;

tread down the wicked in their place. Hide them in the dust together, bind their faces in hidden *darkness*. Then I will also confess to you that **your own right hand can save you**." (Job 40:7–14, emphasis added)

So here it is, God's finger as the probe uncovered the problem. Job, convinced of his own right standing and innocence, had contended with God and tried to correct Him. The light, the understanding he had was not enough, and in his blindness had rebuked God. In the light of God's presence Job saw this was ludicrous, and that he was vile. The surgery continued as the Lord reiterated the proud propositions that had come forth from his servant Job under fire. He had been seeking to annul God's judgment, insisting on his own innocence, and to condemn God in order to justify himself.

The Lord showed him there was a great difficulty here. If Job were in fact to elevate himself as "God," then did he indeed have an arm and voice, splendour and majesty like God's that could react with godly wrath against those who rose up in their independence and dark rebellion against him? Could he look on the proud and humble them, bring them low, in fact, deal with them in righteousness and justice? If he could, then the Lord said he would also confess to Job that his own right hand could save him. Save him from what? Save him from self-righteousness and pride as to think his judgment was more just than God's, and could annul God's judgment.

This passage highlights the vital issues of pride and humility; the pride which is completely independent from God and brings condemnation and death; and the humility which is wholly dependent on God and leads to redemption.

Job's right hand could not save himself.

While his righteousness was not enough and could not save him from separation from God, the seed of Adam's sin in him, if not dealt with, was enough to rob him of God's righteousness and separate him to hell. Job's knowledge was so much less than the tip of an iceberg.

> In Your [God's] light we see light. (Ps 36:9)

In presenting his creation to Job in its sheer magnificence, the Lord was manifesting himself, his incomparable wisdom, love, and righteousness. Proverbs 8 describes the excellence of wisdom:

> "For my mouth will speak truth; wickedness *is* an abomination to my lips. All the words of my mouth *are* with righteousness; nothing crooked or perverse *is* in them. [. . .] For wisdom *is* better than rubies and all the things one may desire cannot be compared with her.
>
> ". . . The fear of the Lord *is* to hate evil; pride and arrogance and the evil way and the perverse mouth I hate. Counsel *is* mine, and sound wisdom; I *am* understanding, I have strength.
>
> [. . .]

> "The Lord possessed me [wisdom] at the beginning of His way, before His works of old. I have been established from everlasting, from the beginning, before there even was an earth. [. . .] Then I was beside Him *as* a master craftsman; and I was daily *His* delight, rejoicing always before Him, rejoicing in His inhabited world, and my delight *was* with the sons of men." (Prov 8:7–8; 11; 13–14; 22–23; 30–31)

This description shows wisdom to be a person. It strikes the same chord as John 1:1–5:

> In the beginning was the Word, and the Word was with God, and the Word was God. [. . .] All things were made through Him, and without Him nothing was made that was made. In Him was life, and the life was the light of men. And the light shines in the darkness, and the darkness did not comprehend [overcome] it.

The darkness did not understand or overcome the light!

In Job's world, there was the darkness of sin; and there was blessing (see footnote in chapter 1 for the literal meaning of bless and curse), but really cursing God in the heart: hypocrisy! Job had offered sacrifices for his children in case they had done just that. Into the world of God's creation, sin, missing God's mark, had become an undeniable factor. Even Job had said, "The earth is given into the hand of the wicked" (Job 9:24).

He was discovering how completely wicked was the hand of the wicked. And his own right hand could not save himself from it. He needed a lifesaver.

Thus, says the Lord:

"Let not the wise *man* glory in his wisdom, let not the mighty *man* glory in his might, nor let the rich *man* glory in his riches; but let him who glories glory in this, that he understands and knows Me, that I *am* the Lord, exercising lovingkindness, judgment [justice], and righteousness in the earth. For in these I delight," declares the Lord. (Jer 9:23–24)

Could it be that God, as Heavenly Father, also had to offer a sacrifice for all his children who had cursed him in their hearts?

The Lord was coming to the conclusion of his personal, guided tour for Job around his creation; a tour that illumined who he is by what he has made. He was preparing Job for a spotlight he was about to shine on Leviathan, an entirely different creature in God's universe.

CHAPTER 6

The Third Spotlight:
On Leviathan—The King of Pride

In no other place in Scripture is almost a whole chapter used to describe one creature (Job 41). God shines a light on Leviathan for Job, just as, at the outset, the Lord had shone a spotlight on Job for the devil. Now, it is as if he is saying to Job, I want you to really consider this fearsome ophidian, so I will describe him to you in detail.

Bible footnotes indicate Leviathan as a large sea creature, exact identity unknown.

A close examination of God's description of Leviathan is vital to get a true picture. The name Leviathan is connected to a coiled, twisted thing, like a wreath.

It sounds almost whimsical the way the Lord began unveiling the essential nature of Leviathan. In Job 41:1, he asked Job if he could fish for him with a hook and line, or a spear. It's as if he opens with:

Can you catch him, and with sweet talk, make him beg you for mercy? (v. 3)

Can you enter into a deal with him and make him your lifelong servant? (s. 4)

How about sporting with him like bird? (v. 5)

Or, put him on a leash like a pet for your children? (v. 5)

Will your friends bargain for him, or make a feast—of him, or for him? (v. 6)

Can he be divided among the buyers? Could he be harpooned like a whale? (v. 7)

Perhaps it is because evil is often joked about, and fun is made of the Ruler of Darkness, that God began his focus on Leviathan in this oddly satirical way.

Perhaps this creature, in roaming to and fro throughout the whole earth, is hunting and fishing for humanity, and uses this very approach himself in order to snare, bring into his net, those who would take him as a joke. Think of Halloween and all the video games along these lines in this day and age—games of power, seduction, conquest, and death.

The prophet Jeremiah said, circa 600 BC, "For death has come through our **windows**, has entered our palaces, to kill off the children—*no longer to be* outside! *And* the young men—*no longer* on the streets!" (Jer. 9:21, emphasis added). It is a warning. Whether by levity or a very heavy *hand*, this creature is an enemy. It is a twisted, coiling serpent, bent on deception, conquest, and death.

The Lord continued in a very serious vein:

> Lay your hand on him; remember the battle—never do it again! Indeed, *any* hope of *overcoming* him is false; shall *one not* be overwhelmed at the sight of him? No one *is so* fierce that he would dare stir him up. (Job 41:8–10).

The Lord presented an uncensored, true image of this massive, ferocious beast that is completely enclosed with impenetrable armour plating. It is impervious to all weapons of warfare. Swords, spears, darts, javelins, arrows, or sling stones are a joke to him, like stubble and straw.

Again, there is a cynical sort of humour to suggest that he may be approached by a double bridle.

> Who can open the doors of his face, *with* his terrible teeth all around? *His* rows of scales are *his* pride, shut up tightly *as with* a seal;
>
> [. . .]
>
> His sneezings flash forth light, and his eyelids *are* like the eyelids of the morning. Out of his mouth go burning lights; sparks of fire shoot out. Smoke goes out of his nostrils, as *from* a boiling pot and burning rushes. His breath kindles coals, and a flame goes out of his mouth. Strength dwells in his neck, and sorrow [despair] dances before him.

[. . .]

His heart is as hard as stone, even as hard as the lower *millstone*. When he raises himself up, the mighty are afraid; because of his crashings they are beside themselves. (Job 41:14–15; 18–22; 24–25)

Out of his nostrils, smoke. And his breath is a fire that sets coals ablaze. This is a dragon! And not just any dragon from a fairy tale.

Here it would be helpful to look at some references from Scripture regarding Leviathan.

> Now the serpent was more cunning than any beast of the field which the Lord God had made. (Gen 3:1)

> For God *is* my king from of old, working salvation in the midst of the earth. You divided the sea by your strength; You broke the heads of the sea serpents in the waters. You broke the heads of Leviathan in pieces . . . (Ps 74:12–14)

> Come my people, enter your chambers, and shut your doors behind you; hide yourself, as it were, for a little moment, until the indignation is passed. For behold the Lord comes out of His place to punish the inhabitants of the earth for their iniquity. The earth also will disclose her blood [shed], and will no more cover her slain.

> In that day, the Lord with His severe sword, great and strong, will punish Leviathan, the fleeing serpent; and He will slay the reptile that *is* in the sea. (Isa 26:20–27:1)

> So, the great dragon was cast out, that serpent of old, called the Devil and Satan, who deceives the whole world . . . (Rev 12:9)

> Then I saw an angel coming down from heaven, having the key to the bottomless pit and a great chain in his hand. He laid hold of the dragon, that

serpent of old, who is *the* Devil and Satan, and bound him for a thousand years . . . (Rev 20:1–2)

The Lord's spotlight on Leviathan in Job 41 concludes in this astonishing way: "On earth there is nothing like him, which is made without fear. He beholds every high *thing*; he *is* king over all the children of pride" (Job 41:33–34). The NIV version says: "Nothing on earth is his equal—a creature without fear. He looks down on all that are haughty; he is king over all that are proud." In the NIV of verse 34, even the phrase "He looks down on" creates an image of arrogance. This is pride personified. And according to God, he is the king over all who are proud.

Who are the proud? Only all those who, like Adam and Eve, chose to believe and obey the voice of the serpent over the voice of God. And so, as Paul said in Romans 11:32, "God has committed them all to disobedience, that He might have mercy on all."

The terrible truth is that humankind's fall meant that all people fell into the power and likeness of the devil, being proudly independent from God. They would be stamped with his image, instead of the Creator God's image, who made them. So, on earth there is nothing like Leviathan for pride, power, rebellion, and disobedience toward God. Unless God orchestrated the terrible trial, by which all the pride in Job came to the surface and ran out, Job would unknowingly have those dark attributes within, which would one day mark him out as a subject of the "king over all who are proud" (Job 41:34).

Although nothing on earth is Leviathan's equal, there is one who is immeasurably more powerful than he. In this spotlight on Leviathan in Job 41, God shines a stunning beam of light once more on Himself. This appears in Job 41:10–11 (emphasis added):

> No one *is so* fierce that he would dare stir him up. **Who then is able to stand against Me?** Who has preceded Me, that I should repay *him*? **Everything under heaven is Mine.**

The enemy is mighty, but the Lord is mightier beyond comparison! "The earth *is* the Lord's and all its fullness, the world and those who dwell therein" (Ps 24:1). Although it was given into the hands of the devil through Adam and Eve's sin, God had a plan right from the beginning, a plan of redemption. The seed of the woman, "will bruise your head, and you shall bruise His heel" (Gen 3:15). This refers to the Son of God crushing Satan's head, as he, Jesus, died on the cross of Calvary—had his heel crushed there—but he overcame death, because it could not hold him. He was the willing, sinless substitute, sacrificed in our place.

God the Father, out of love for the world, offered up God the Son, who gave himself willingly to redeem all sinful, lost humankind.

> And being found in appearance as a man, He humbled Himself and became obedient to *the point of* death, even the death of the cross. (Phil 2:8)

> For He made Him who knew no sin *to be* sin for us,
> that we might become the righteousness of God in
> Him. (2 Cor 5:21)

God did not want robots who would have to obey him,
programmed to obey him, so he made them in his holy
image with the freedom to choose trust and obedience, or
independence and disobedience.

With this freedom, Lucifer and a third of the angels chose
rebellion and disobedience, and determined to take all God's
people, too. Isaiah the prophet showed Lucifer's rebellion:

> "How you are fallen from heaven, O Lucifer, son of
> the morning! *How* you are cut down to the ground,
> you who weakened the nations! For you have said
> in your heart: 'I will ascend into heaven, I will exalt
> my throne above the stars of God; I will also sit on
> the mount of the congregation on the farthest sides
> of the north; I will ascend above the heights of the
> clouds, I will be like the Most High.' Yet you will
> be brought down to Sheol, to the lowest depth of
> the Pit.
>
> "Those who see you will gaze at you, *and* consider
> you, *saying*: '*Is* this the man who made the earth
> tremble, who shook kingdoms, who made the
> world as a wilderness and destroyed its cities, *who*
> did not open the house of its prisoners [would not
> let his prisoners go home]?'" (Isa 14:12–17)

C. S. Lewis, in his book *Perelandra*, wrote about Bent Eldila (angels). He showed that, tragically, some of the angels, in rebelling against their Creator, became twisted with arrant iniquity—hence the absolute bent to evil. They missed the mark of what their Maker intended for them.

> You [Lucifer] *were* perfect in your ways from the day you were created, till iniquity was found in you. (Ezek. 28:15)

Iniquity means the essence of wrong-doing or evil, the "bent" to sin.

There are three "I's" in the word iniquity: the unholy trinity of "I," which is at the heart of Leviathan's twisted ambition.

His five 'I will's in Isaiah 14:13–15 show his unmistakable desire and design to replace Almighty God and ruin his creation, and the pinnacle of his creation, which is human-kind itself.

He did usurp Adam and Eve's place of authority on earth. This is seen when he tempted Jesus in the wilderness:

> Then the devil, taking Him up on a high moun-tain, showed Him all the kingdoms of the world in a moment of time. And the devil said to Him, "All this authority I will give You, and their glory; for *this* has been delivered to me, and I give it to whomever I wish. Therefore, if You will worship before me, all will be Yours." (Luke 4:5–7)

Carried away by his own conceits, the devil was convinced he had the power to overcome Jesus, the Son of God, who became Son of Man, for the purpose of humankind's redemption.

Jesus replied, "Get behind me Satan! For it is written, 'You shall worship the Lord your God and Him only you shall serve'" (Luke 4:8). This was at the outset of Jesus's earthly ministry prior to his coming out of the wilderness after forty days of fasting. Just before the completion of Jesus's work on earth, he said to his disciples, "I will no longer talk much with you, for the ruler of this world is coming and he has nothing [no hold] in Me" (John 14:30). Because Jesus had no personal sin in him, the devil had no power or claim over him. No one could convict Jesus of sin (see John 8:46).

This could not be said of any other human being. Even the best of human beings has this bent to independence from God, which is inbred pride. The nature to sin, which is iniquity, has been downloaded in every human heart since the serpent successfully tempted Adam and Eve. The ultimate end of this degeneration of Lucifer become Leviathan, become the accuser, the king over all the sons of pride, is the pointing of his finger—before God—and saying, "he's mine, she is mine, they are *all* mine, of all God's creation!"

For with You *is* the fountain of Life;
in Your light we see light. (Psalm 36:9)

CHAPTER 7

The Fourth Spotlight

He saved them from the hand of him who hated *them*, and redeemed them from the hand of the enemy. (Ps 106:10)

Job *got* it. He stood transparent before God, humble and repentant.

Then Job answered the Lord and said:

"I know that You can do everything, and that no purpose *of Yours* can be withheld from You. *You asked*, 'Who is this who hides counsel without knowledge?' Therefore I have uttered what I did not understand, things too wonderful for me, which I did not know. Listen, please, and let me speak; *You said*, 'I will question you, and you shall answer Me.'

"I have heard of You by the hearing of the ear, but now my eye sees You. Therefore I abhor *myself*, and repent in dust and ashes." (Job 42:1–6)

Pride had gone; this humble child of God understood the *why*—why he had needed such an excruciating trial. Nothing else could have separated him from the damning ingredients within that had made him a subject of the king of pride.

> And so it was, after the Lord had spoken these words to Job, that the Lord said to Eliphaz the Temanite, "My wrath is aroused against you and your two friends, for **you have not spoken of Me what is right, as My servant Job has**." (Job 42:7, emphasis added)

Years ago, when I read these words, the thought came to mind, "But Lord, Job said you had denied him justice." And I felt the Lord's answer was: "I *did* deny him justice! *I gave him mercy instead!*"

Wow! Justice, even for Job, would have brought condemnation. I was filled with amazement at the mercy and plan of God. Truly he is the Heavenly Father who foreknew he would need to offer the perfect sacrifice for his children. Children who had, and would, "bless" God in their hearts, but in truth, curse him and themselves with their hidden, often unrecognized hypocrisy. To not speak right about God is the most heinous of crimes. It is truly the legacy of Lucifer turned Leviathan. Here the Lord turned this fourth spotlight on Eliphaz, Bildad, and Zophar for this sin of theirs—not speaking right about God. This had caused Job such grief, and now raised the wrath of the Lord against them for their ignominy. He issued their marching orders:

> Now therefore, take for yourselves seven bulls and
> seven rams, go to My servant Job, and offer up for
> yourselves a burnt offering; and My servant Job
> shall pray for you. For I will accept him, lest I deal
> with you *according to your* folly; because you have
> not spoken of Me *what is* right, as My servant Job
> *has*. (Job 42:8)

In this direct injunction, the Lord mentioned "My servant
Job" three times. In the end, as at the beginning, God
affirmed Job as his servant. The friends had not spoken
of God what was right, while Job had. The Lord always
does what is right; he had the three friends come to Job to
present their burnt offerings to God before him, in order
that Job could intercede for them. The Lord had already
determined to accept Job's prayer. It was inescapably hum-
bling for Eliphaz, Bildad, and Zophar to comply. By the
grace and love of God, it was also very freeing, because by
so doing, they would not be dealt with by God according to
their folly.

It was also the moment of truth and freedom for Job.
Forgiveness is the foremost requirement in the family of
God. In order to be forgiven by God, we must forgive as he
forgives us, no ifs, ands, buts, or hidden clauses.

> So, Eliphaz the Temanite and Bildad the Shuhite
> *and* Zophar the Naamathite went and did as the
> Lord commanded them; for the Lord had accepted
> Job. And the Lord restored Job's losses when he
> prayed for his friends. Indeed, the Lord gave Job
> twice as much as he had before. (Job 42:9–10)

As family and friends gathered around him and showered him with gifts and consolation, perhaps it was like the lifting of a long period of social distancing after a pandemic! And, if there was any doubt as to who had brought about the terrible ordeal, the text makes it very clear: "for all the adversity that the Lord had brought upon him" (Job 42:11). In fact, the spotlights on Job, God, Leviathan, the friends, and the grave indictment against them—all this was directly of God.

There was a foreign body buried deep in the soul of God's creation. Without its total removal, it would result in poisoning and absolute demise. It engendered grumbling and complaint against God and his order.

A passage in James 5:9–11 helps here:

> Do not grumble against one another, . . . lest you be condemned. Behold, the Judge is standing at the door! . . . take the prophets, who spoke in the name of the Lord, as an example of suffering and patience. Indeed, we count them blessed who endure. You have heard of the perseverance of Job and seen the end *intended* by the Lord—that the Lord is very compassionate and merciful.

In the midst of his darkness and desolation, faith had risen up in Job, causing him to cry, "I know that my Redeemer lives" (Job 19:25).

The end intended by the Lord was overwhelming and magnificent redemption. The Lord poured blessing upon blessing on Job. He doubled all his livestock: 14,000 sheep; 6,000 camels, 1,000 yoke of oxen, and 1,000 female donkeys. He also gave him seven sons and three beautiful daughters. At first sight, it looked as though he stopped short of the "doubling" when it came to the children. It was Bible teacher Derek Prince who gave wonderful, encouraging insight into the matter of the children. He said the Lord "only" gave another seven sons and three daughters because he had heard Job's prayers, and received his sacrifices for his first seven sons and three daughters. They were safe in the arms of God! And so, in giving ten more children, He actually did double Job's offspring. Amazing, redeeming love! Job's lovely daughters, replete with colourful beauty and fragrance, were blessed by their dad with an inheritance along with their brothers.

Job lived 140 more years, enjoying his children and grandchildren through four generations. "So Job died, old and full of days" (Job 42:17). The operation was a complete success!

BRIDGE

Job was the Lord's servant at the beginning and end. Even so, he had only heard about God at first. He needed to see God! We who have heard of God, and on that basis serve him, also need to meet and see God. How is that possible, in our day? In John 14:9, Jesus said, "He who has seen Me has seen the Father."

But later, after the resurrection, Jesus said to Thomas, "Thomas, because you have seen Me, you have believed. Blessed *are* those who have not seen and *yet* have believed" (John 20:29).

Therefore, we need to "see" Jesus by faith. Paul, in Romans 10:17, said: "So then faith *comes* by hearing, and hearing by the word of God."

Finally, we will see God's spotlight on the Son of God in his Word. Here again we have such effulgence. How can we gaze at the sun and not be blinded? We need to gaze at the Son of God, and have our darkness turned to light.

The Father said, "This is My beloved Son. Hear Him!" (Mark 9:7).

CHAPTER 8

The Fifth Spotlight

The Fifth Spotlight on God the Son—Forethought, *not* Afterthought!

> For it pleased *the Father that* in Him all the fullness should dwell, and by Him to reconcile all things to Himself, by Him, whether things on earth or things in heaven, having made peace through the blood of His cross. (Col 1:19–20)

God talked about "My servant Job" at the beginning and end of the book that bears his name. There were sacrifices offered at the beginning by Job efficaciously for his children, to set them on the right path. At the end, the Lord required the friends to offer a burnt offering of seven bulls and seven rams for themselves. Seven is the number of perfection. Was this a type of perfect sacrifice God had foreordained to set his wayward children on the right path? Scripture says: "without shedding of blood there is no remission [forgiveness of sin]" (Heb 9:22).

Missing the mark of God's purpose is so serious as to end up completely out of his "picture." There is a price to pay for redemption. Job, the best of men, needed a Redeemer, and so does the whole human race, for reasons already discussed.

There is a hidden piece to this puzzle that now needs a spotlight shone on it. This hidden piece is the redemption price for the whole world. Here is another conundrum: How can a spotlight be shone on the one who said, "I am the light of the world" (John 8:12)? This again is obviously metaphor.

The Greek word *afikomen* means "the Coming One," or *habba* in Hebrew. It is a clear reference to the expected Jewish Messiah. In the Jewish Passover Seder, remembering and celebrating the Israelites' deliverance from enslavement in Egypt, a piece of the matzah bread, which is unleavened (yeast represents sin), pierced, and scored, is broken. Part of it is wrapped in a cloth and hidden. Later it is looked for and found, usually by children, then given to everyone and eaten as the final morsel (from *Mysterious Passover Symbols* by David Brickner).

Although hidden from many Jewish people at this time, it is seen as representing Jesus the Messiah. At the Last Supper, he took bread, gave thanks, broke it, and gave it to his disciples just prior going to the cross of Calvary in our place. It was there his body was whipped and pierced, then later wrapped in a shroud, and hidden away in a tomb. At the Last Supper, he said the unleavened bread represented his body, which was broken for us.

The Bible is replete with pictures of God's plan of redemption, written and proclaimed for centuries. Here are some of them from the Old and New Testaments.

> In the beginning was the Word, and the Word was with God, and the Word was God. He was in the beginning with God. All things were made through Him, and without Him nothing was made that was made. In Him was life, and the life was the light of men. And the light shines in the darkness, and the darkness did not comprehend it. (John 1:1–5)

John went on to say, in 1:14, "And the Word became flesh and dwelt among us, and we beheld His glory, the glory as of the only begotten of the Father, full of grace and truth."

When Lucifer became Leviathan and seemed to sabotage and derail God's plan, God, all-knowing, had a deeper plan:

> And I will put enmity between you and the woman, and between your seed and her Seed. He shall bruise your head, and you shall bruise His heel. (Gen 3:15)

> The people who walked in darkness have seen a great light; those who dwelt in the land of the shadow of death, upon them a light has shined.

> [. . .]

> For unto us a Child is born, unto us a Son is given; and the government will be upon His shoulder. And His name will be called Wonderful, Counselor,

Mighty God, Everlasting Father, Prince of Peace. Of the increase of *His* government and peace *there will be* no end, upon the throne of David and over His Kingdom, to order it and establish it with judgment and justice from that time forward, even forever. The zeal of the Lord of hosts will perform this" (Isa 9:2; 6–7).

Now the birth of Jesus Christ was as follows: After His mother Mary was betrothed to Joseph, before they came together, she was found with child of the Holy Spirit. Then Joseph her husband, being a just *man*, and not wanting to make her a public example, was minded to put her away secretly. But while he thought about these things, behold, an angel of the Lord appeared to him in a dream, saying, "Joseph, son of David, do not be afraid to take to you Mary your wife, for that which is conceived in her is of the Holy Spirit. And she will bring forth a Son, and you shall call His name Jesus, for He will save His people from their sins."

So all this was done that it might be fulfilled which was spoken by the Lord through the prophet, saying: "Behold, the virgin shall be with child, and bear a Son, and you shall call His name Immanuel," which is translated, "God with us." (Matt 1:18–23)

"But when the fullness of time had come, God sent forth His Son, born of a woman, born under the law, to redeem those who were under the law, that we might receive the adoption as sons" (Gal 4:4–5).

The woman to whom the Son of God was born was Mary. She was of the tribe of Judah. When the patriarch, Jacob, son of Isaac, grandson of Abraham, was about to die, he blessed his sons and prophesied over them. Of Judah, he said, "The scepter shall not depart from Judah, nor the lawgiver from between his feet, until Shiloh comes; and to him *shall be* the obedience of the people" (Gen 49:10). Shiloh is described in *Young's Concordance* as: "A description of Messiah, as the Prince of Peace; or as the 'seed' of Judah."

Micah prophesied:

> "But you Bethlehem Ephrathah, *though* you are little among the thousands of Judah, *yet* out of you shall come forth to Me the One to be Ruler in Israel, whose goings forth *are* from of old, from everlasting" (Mic 5:2).

> "Rejoice greatly, O daughter of Zion! Shout, O daughter of Jerusalem! Behold, your King is coming to you; He is just and having salvation, lowly and riding on a donkey, a colt, the foal of a donkey." (Zech. 9:9)

> Now when they drew near to Jerusalem, and came to Bethphage at the Mount of Olives, then Jesus sent two disciples, saying to them, "Go into the village opposite you, and immediately you will find a donkey tied, and a colt with her. Loose *them* and bring *them* to Me. And if anyone says anything to you, you shall say, 'The Lord has need of them,' and immediately he will send them."

All this was done that it might be fulfilled which was spoken by the prophet, saying:

"Tell the daughter of Zion, 'Behold, your King is coming to you, lowly, and sitting on a donkey, a colt, the foal of a donkey.'" (Matt 21:1–5)

Psalms 22 and 69, written by King David about 1000 years before Christ's Incarnation, have direct prophecies that were precisely fulfilled in the crucifixion and death of Jesus Christ.

Isaiah 53, written circa 700 BC, is another amazing prophecy, breathtaking in its accuracy about the suffering servant Messiah. For example, 53:3–6:

He is despised and rejected by men, a Man of sorrows and acquainted with grief. And we hid, as it were *our* faces from Him; He was despised, and we did not esteem Him.

Surely, He has borne our griefs [sicknesses] and carried our sorrows [pains]; yet we esteemed Him stricken, smitten by God and afflicted. But He *was* wounded for our transgressions, He *was* bruised for our iniquities; the chastisement [punishment] for our peace *was* upon Him, and by His stripes [blows that cut in] we are healed. All we like sheep have gone astray; we have turned, every one, to his own way; and the Lord has laid on Him the iniquity of us all."

To accomplish reconciliation between God and all his sin-defiled creation, it required the completely sinless sacrifice of Jesus, God's Son, and his blood shed on the cross. This alone brought peace.

Lucifer can mean day star. Jesus is "the Root and the Offspring of David, the Bright and Morning Star" referred to in Revelation 22:16.

Daystar and Bright and Morning Star—this could bring confusion.

Lucifer fell from his exalted position as guardian cherub of the earth and became Satan, the twisted, tempting serpent, and the accuser: counsel for the prosecution.

Jesus, the only begotten of the Father, the Word of God, through whom all things were made, became the seed of the woman who would crush the serpent's head (Gen 3:15).

Two historical accounts, one from Numbers 21:4–9, and the other from John's Gospel 3:1–21, bring into sharp focus God's wonderful love for his erring children, and his plan of salvation.

The Israelites again and again grumbled against God and Moses on the journey from Egypt back to Canaan, the Promised Land. This time, their complaint mushroomed into full-blown rebellion. God had supernaturally provided food for them which they called manna, but when they were discouraged, their attitude became one of loathing God's heavenly manna bread, to the point of calling it "worthless" (Num 21:5)! "So, the Lord sent fiery serpents" into their midst (Num 21:6). Many of the hateful grumblers were bitten, and many died. The people realized they had sinned grievously, biting the hand that fed and saved them, so they admitted they had sinned, and begged Moses to intercede on their behalf for the Lord to take away the serpents.

> Then the Lord said to Moses: "Make a fiery *serpent* and set it on a pole; it shall be that everyone who is bitten, when he looks at it, shall live." So, Moses made a bronze serpent, and put it on a pole; and so it was, if a serpent had bitten anyone, when he looked at the bronze serpent, he lived. (Num 21:8–9)

About 1,400 years later, a Pharisee named Nicodemus came to visit Jesus under the cover of darkness. He was a teacher of Israel, but he was in for some of his greatest life lessons. He quickly found out from Jesus that unless he was "born again," neither he nor anyone else could see the kingdom of God. Nicodemus was completely baffled by this, and understood Jesus to be speaking literally. He discovered from Jesus it was not a matter of going back into his mother's womb, but rather a new birth by water and the Spirit; baptism, indicating a death to the old life, and being given a new life, filled with and led by the Holy Spirit of God: Holy Spirit, the Wind of God, and Fire of God blowing and going where he wills.

As Nicodemus struggled to get on the right wavelength, Jesus said:

No one has ascended to heaven but He who came down from heaven, *that is*, the Son of Man [Jesus often referred to himself by this title] Who is in heaven. And as Moses lifted up the serpent in the wilderness, even so must the Son of Man be lifted up [indicating crucifixion], that whoever believes in Him should not perish but have eternal life. For God so loved the world that He gave His only begotten Son, that whoever believes in Him should not perish but have everlasting life. For God did not send His Son into the world to condemn the world, but that the world through Him might be saved. (John 3:13–17)

Nicodemus needed to understand that every complainer and grumbler against God who does not speak right about God is dying from the serpent's deadly bite. But here is the antidote:

"God so loved the world that He gave his only begotten Son . . ." (John 3:16)

For He made Him [Jesus, his Son] who knew no sin *to be* sin for us, that we might become the righteousness of God in Him. (2 Cor 5:21)

If we look and believe, we will be healed of Leviathan's bite of iniquity!

Jesus was lifted up on the cross to pay the penalty for our sin—the ransom price. But because he himself was without sin, death could not hold him, and the third day after burial, he rose from the dead.

The Scriptures testify that he appeared to his disciples many days before ascending back to his Father in heaven. He talked and ate with them, and Jesus himself shone a light on Old Testament Scriptures that referred to him. The story is found in Luke 24:13–27. He drew alongside two of his disciples on the Emmaus road, on the day of his resurrection. Their eyes were kept from recognizing him. He asked what they were discussing as they walked along. They were obviously sad, having witnessed his crucifixion only days earlier. They thought he must be a stranger if he had not heard about the things that had happened in Jerusalem during those days.

And He said to them, "What things?"

So, they said to Him, "The things concerning Jesus of Nazareth, who was a Prophet mighty in deed and word before God and all the people, and how the chief priests and our rulers delivered Him to be condemned to death, and crucified Him. But we were hoping that He was going to redeem Israel. Indeed, besides all this, today is the third day since these things happened. Yes, and certain women of our company, who arrived at the tomb early, astonished us. When they did not find His body, they came saying that they had also seen a vision of angels who said He was alive. And certain of those *who were* with us went to the tomb and found *it* just as the women had said; but Him they did not see."

Then He said to them, "O foolish ones, and slow of heart to believe all that the prophets have spoken! Ought not the Christ [Messiah] to have suffered these things and to enter into His glory?" And beginning at Moses, and the Prophets, He expounded to them in all the Scriptures [Old Testament] the things concerning Himself. (Luke 24:19–27)

Why do bad things happen to good people? Why does God let—make—bad things happen to good people? Why did God make the worst things happen to the best of people, to Jesus, his own Son?

Now from the sixth hour until the ninth hour there was darkness over the land. And about the ninth hour Jesus cried out with a loud voice, saying, "Eli, Eli, lama sabachthani?" that is "My God, My God, **why** have You forsaken Me?"

Some of those who stood there, when they heard *that*, said, "This Man is calling for Elijah!" Immediately one of them ran and took a sponge, filled *it* with sour wine and put *it* on a reed, and offered it to Him to drink.

The rest said, "Let Him alone; let us see if Elijah will come to save Him."

And Jesus cried out again with a loud voice, and yielded up His spirit.

> Then, behold, the veil of the temple was torn in two from top to bottom . . . (Matt 27:45–51, emphasis added).

This passage from Matthew includes quotes from David's Psalm 22:1 and Psalm 69:21, showing the fulfillment of those prophecies.

"My God, My God, why have you forsaken me?"

This is the "why" cry of the Lamb of God! "Lama" is the Hebrew word for "why," and the reason for his anguished "why" here was because Jesus, the Son of God, in his agony on the cross, was suffering the greatest agony of all, which was *separation* from his Father God, which he had never known before.

When in his torn body he breathed his last as the Son of Man, the mighty, thick veil of the temple in Jerusalem, which separated the holy place from the holy of holies (the most holy place where God's presence was), was torn in two from top to bottom. This surely was the Heavenly Father's reply to his Son's substitutional death in our place: Jesus had tasted and experienced humanity's separation from God.

His Father tore the separating veil (the "door") from top to bottom, indicating the way was now open back into His presence.

Jesus said he was "the door of the sheep," in John 10:7. Now the door was opened for all who look to him to come back home. Unholiness had shut the door. Holiness had reopened it. The hands of God the Son, stretched out on the cross, had accomplished his work.

Why wouldn't Holy God stretch out his hands to touch, curse Job and the rest of us?

> The arms and hands of God stretched out
> to embrace the world, the returning prodigals.
> His hands and feet, whole body humbled and laid down
> to receive the penalty for sin; His heart
> poured out to close the gap; His body
> cursed – for it is written: "Cursed *is* everyone
> who hangs on a tree." (Gal 3:13)
> Cursed for Job, and you and me –
> And all because He loves us.
> God denied me justice. And gave me mercy instead!

"Would you indeed annul My judgment? Would you condemn Me that you may be justified?" (Job 40:8). Job could not condemn God that he may be justified. But God could condemn himself in his sinless yet sin-bearing Son on the Cross, to justify us!

Jesus said: "Because I live, you will live also" (John 14:19).

ACKNOWLEDGEMENTS

I wish to thank those who have encouraged me along the way. Thanks to my husband, Friedhelm, who typed out the manuscript and whose face sometimes lit up as he reviewed the chapters; he made my face light up too, when, on busy days, he stood in as head cook and bottle washer. Thank you, Matthew for your great pen and ink sketches; and Esther, your beloved, Tobias and Jackson for loaning husband and Daddy out of your busy lives.

Thanks to Douglas and Peggy Scott who said, "You have to write it down."

Many thanks to all the good friends who contributed in so many ways: Dean Hull, Erik Reimer and Jim Seagram, whose brotherly friendship and counsel is like pure gold.

Thanks to Joy Shin, our Korean daughter, who often hiked with me in God's classroom, where we discussed the "treasures of darkness."

Thank you, David's House of Prayer family for all your prayers and encouragement, including Cathi and Bruce

Guenter who were the first to read God on the Job with us in Life Group.

Special thanks to Chrissie and Randy Emerson and your whole family, who know what this is all about, and who echo Job's, "I know that my Redeemer lives".

I'm grateful to Rayna and John Stone who pointed us in the direction of Friesen Press; and to Sandy Tillyer, who really prayed about that. And thank you to all the Friesen Press Team who have so ably guided us along the launch path. Kayla Lang, my Publishing Specialist, deserves a special accolade. What would I have done without you? Thank you!

ENDORSEMENTS

Joyce did not ask me to write this endorsement because of my involvement in theological education for over twenty years. She asked me because we are friends and she knew I would "speak rightly of her."

Similarly, I believe God prompted Joyce to write this commentary not because of any theological pedigree, but because she has been a friend of God over the years and has spent countless hours at the feet of Jesus, listening to him teach.

The rich insights contained in this commentary have been gleaned from those hours spent face to face in his Presence. May these insights lead you not merely to conclusions about the book of Job; may they lead you to the Author himself.

Erik Reimer

Joyce has written with clear insight, deep revelation and nuanced humour, an inspiring review of the mystery of human suffering, spiritual pride and Divine grace. This book is for the astute student of scripture and in every chapter, one finds the Holy Spirit revealing the nature of humanity, evil and redemption. When you read and absorb this book, you will be profoundly changed forever! This is a piercing, yet uplifting book, written by a faithful and gifted author on the most challenging topic known to humankind.

Well done! Praise God!

The Rev. Jim Seagram: former priest and forever a friend and brother in Christ of Joyce Jungclaus

Joyce is a spiritual Canadian mother and I am her Korean daughter. Since 2012, she has shared some insightful ideas with me during our hikes in the beauty of His nature.

The stories in this book were introduced to me eight years ago. The metaphorical usage of the word "spotlight" in contextualizing underlying themes of Job in the Bible, is delicately structured and inspiring.

I sincerely hope that you'll have the pleasure of knowing God, who blesses us with the utmost meaning of life through this valuable piece of work.

Joy Shin

I have known Joyce for years. I never met anyone who endeavoured to live out their life, by walking with Jesus every minute, as well as she does. I am amazed at her grasp of scripture and always refer to her when I need to find a passage in the Bible. She is consistent in her prayer walk, sings praise as sweetly as anyone ever did, and turns every decision over to God. Proud to call her one of my mentors.

Dean Hull

Printed in Canada